My Dads & Me
coloring book

Created by Mark Loewen

Celebrating LGBT Families - Vol. 2

BQB

Virginia

My Dads & Me Coloring Book
Celebrating LGBT Families - Vol. 2
© 2020 Mark Loewen. All rights reserved.

This is a work of fiction. All of the products of the author's imagination or are used fictitiously.

Published in the United States by BQB Publishing
(an imprint of Boutique of Quality Books Publishing Company)
www.bqbpublishing.com

Printed in the United States of America
978-1-945448-91-1 (p)

For cover and interior illustrations, author worked with an illustrator who chose to remain anonymous.
Interior Design Setup: Robin Krauss, www.bookformatters.com

What is the True Color of Family?

When I was a kid, I thought all families had to have one mom and one dad. But then I fell in love with a boy and we became a family. And, when we adopted our daughter, we became a family of three. We were so happy!

Some people were very confused. They thought only families with one mom and one dad could be truly happy. They never met a family like ours, which is crazy because families like ours are everywhere!

I created this coloring book so everyone could see that all families can be just as happy if they love each other.

Do you want to help me get the word out? You can share your colored pages online. Just tag me (@markloewen.author) or use #Truecolorsoffamily.

Together, we'll show the world that the true color of family is LOVE!

Sincerely,
Mark Loewen

Other books by Mark Loewen

What Does a Princess Really Look Like?
The True Colors of a Princess Coloring Book
The True Colors of Family Coloring Book

About the Author

Mark Loewen is a dad, a psychotherapist, and a children's author. He was born in Asuncion, Paraguay and moved to the United States to pursue his counseling career. He met the love of his life shortly after finishing graduate school. A few years later, they became dads through open adoption.

Mark's passion for equality drives everything he does, whether he is in the role of husband, father, therapist, or friend. Through his books, Mark hopes to add more representation of diverse families into kid's literature. He is the author of the children's book, *What Does a Princess Really Look Like?*, the companion coloring book, *The True Colors of a Princess*, and *The True Colors of Family Coloring Book*, which is the first book in this series.

To create this coloring book, Mark worked with an illustrator who chose to remain anonymous.

To learn more about Mark and his books, visit www.markloewenauthor.com